Seven Robins

SEVEN ROBINS

Neile Graham

Penumbra Press, 1983

Published by PENUMBRA PRESS, P.O. Box 340, Moonbeam,
Ontario, Canada POL 1V0 with financial assistance from
The Canada Council and The Ontario Arts Council.

ISBN 0 920806 55 4

For Robin and Dick

Inside the river, rocks roll over
And disclose their dark, wet unders.
Beneath them, everything dies of travel and light.

J. Michael Yates

Imagine a forest
A real forest.

W.S. Graham

One

Tuesday. I wish it were
any other day —
the rain never stops, it
snaps against the
window like a stranger
watching in.

Wednesday. Today
I can't move,
the cottage shifts
under my feet,
I know outside
will be wild, the wind
is a beast shaking the house
as I write, watching
for the smallest sign.

Thursday. I
went outside, and brought
fallen boughs of fir
to the fire. It is
warm, and the wood burning
brings the scent of the
forest in.
I couldn't bring myself
to write more than a note
asking you to come.

Friday. Today
the mail came with
no letters. I put your
note in the fire,
watched it flare.
I turned to the
window to see
the crows harass
a hawk, was glad
when he drew them away.

Saturday.
I can't remember.

Already Sunday.
My radio barely draws
the music in, I measure
it drifting. I went outside,
was held by the sound
of rain on the leaves, but
escaped inside.

Monday. I had a strange
dream last night
that I was a small
animal in a shell, it
made me realize
my days are round
and slow. Inside them
I move like an embryo.

you are writing from this
far place pouring
ink from one hand
scotch from the other

the messages you send
are beyond reply

by day you wander
through the barking crowds
barter for your dinner

the days run over you
like wild dogs—
such a tangle of warm limbs
scrambling and gone

already it is night
and you're in solitude
the trees are hard
voices of strangers
knocking against your window

IN REPLY TO YOUR LETTER

I'm sorry this letter has been
slow to reach you:
this is because words
do not smuggle cheaply,
but exact their own price.
They leave little of me here.

I write now while
my children and husband
roam the mountain hunting dry wood
and fire.
From the basket beside me
my new-born smells of sleep
and vague dreams.

The questions in your last letter
I can hardly answer.
How I am:
I am how the rain falls.
We live in a cloud
on our mountain,
where the rain doesn't fall,
but is.
This is how I am.

How I miss you: I tell you now
these are the first words I've spent;
they carry more than their weight
to you.

AFTER A LONG SILENCE

I lose myself in this March forest,
weary now, aching for sleep.

The month won't end, I won't find
my way through it. My bones crumble.

My writing crumbles. I keep wondering
where the light is coming from.

Words won't approach, only the silence
will and does. The words have a better place.

                    *

I'm walking south.
The trees bend before me.

Silence taps me on the shoulder,
and I turn to read his lips:

Where have you come from?
Where are you going?

I talk because I have
nothing to say.

                    *

I will have more to say.
The words will return.

Or better still, I will catch
the poem going past a fir.

And where will I go?
Wherever he's been.

What will I find there?
Bits of his coat tail,

his collar, a sleeve, silence
blocking my path.

How can I get past him? Only how
the month does.

I will slip away while he's busy
looking for the shape of me.

WE ARE STILL IN THE WRITING

for Robin Skelton

Looking for some kind of light
we find each other in this cave,
this birthing dark.
We check our pockets for candles
or matches, finding neither
we link hands and push our way
through the darkness.
Our footsteps are a dull echo
we barely hear. We can travel
only forward. Envisioning
faces unmasked by the darkness,
we discover our own faces,
our own hands checking our pockets
for candles and light.

Melt the wax from a hard
nameless block, *go liquid.*
Use your child's crayon for
colour, add your cheap perfume,
throw it all in. Do it all at
once, pull the wicks taut
in the frames and molds. *Tighter.*
Dip the frames, keep the
rest liquid and pour
into the molds, *through
your hands. Pour into
the mold, go liquid.*

Fire builds dreams;
I built a fire, placed
stones around it
numberless as night.
My strange manufacture
grows as boys do, stretching
in their sleep.
    I sleep
to dream, but so lightly now
I envision only myself,
sleeping.

The fire at the centre
ravels the nights. I hold my hands
to the shape of the flames,
catch their light on my fingers,
and find myself bound here by fire,
as men, sleeping, are bound
by cumbersome dreams.

DEAR CHRISTINA

I keep reading the poem you left me
again and again; like the passion fruit
I have found no one to share it.
They wait on the shelf: talismans, promises.

I went walking yesterday up and down the hill.
At seven when I woke the light had been spreading,
the moon still choking on the fog,
then the path dusty despite
the damp of the morning. I walked for hours,
felt as though I had never walked anywhere.

Now I am sitting in my bed. Around me
the house mumbles, settling into night.
The cat is warm beside me, with his
monkey paws curled around his head;
his tail twitches in sleep.
There is something I should do.

When I walked yesterday all the trees
looked the same. I thought that they followed me
along the path, stopping whenever I glanced up.
I tried to trick them into moving as I watched,
but failed.

There is so little news:
the Eurinyes have been tamed by Athena,
Virgil and Dante have reached the Whip of Sloth,
Gogol has torn his wife to pieces.
My cat has a nightmare
and the trees walked with me.

I looked at a picture of you today
and I swear I saw a passion fruit in your hand
like a talisman.
I will read the poem again.

FU DOGS

These dogs sit heavily
in my dreams;
their serpent faces,
guarding, keep all
other faces from my dreams.

They bring me
good luck. I
can't say that
isn't enough.

They hate each other,
are not really a pair.
One is larger, his belly and legs
covered with spots of blood.
The other is smaller, wiry,
and has blood only on his jaws.

I dream
they are walking.
One continually turns
to nip the other,
who can only snap back.

They hate each other;
they use all
the bad luck
to wish on each other,
leaving only good
for me. But their hate
leaves a harmony
and when they wait in dreams
they wait together.

RECIPE

The mug still warm but
empty. Light pulling
from the windows, the
wind is just beginning
to boil in the trees.

When you come back to
this room, you'll sense it.
There is something in
what I've written here
to send you away,

a spell in the fire
not yet lit, in the
liquid drunk, and the
storm just ready to
brew again. Outside.

Don't speak: imagine
you have forgotten what you
came here for;
imagine you can understand
me when I say you must
begin again; imagine that you
do, that you are
waking again this morning,
but that you
are in a different room
and everything is not where
you left it. Objects have
changed colour and position;
the food in the fridge is foreign
and your clothes don't
fit. Imagine going
out into a different street
where even the lines on the
sidewalk are different. Retrace
the steps that have led you
here, imagine you walk into
this room and I say, Don't speak.

RIVER

When I first arrived here I saw there were only
two directions: up and down river. A compass
would point out no other course. There was nothing
much here but the river, and the weather was always
river. I remember when I asked the man gathering
trout the time of day, he glanced at his watch, and
replied, *River.*

I let my feet slip into the river, but was not sure
how to pull them out. I decided to pan for gold,
but the river hid the sand where I could reach it
only by throwing myself to the water. I hesitated
for a moment, then happened to glance upriver where
I saw that the trout had hooked the man and drawn
him in among them for the river to feed on.

I could not feel my legs, and was frightened to
look at them, to watch the river running over them,
bending and shortening them. I began to long for
land, but the smoothed, steep stone of the banks
had long surrendered to the river, and would let
me fall to it. I found my growing thirst hard to
resist, and I rested my face in the water.

The river runs fuller this year, and I travel in
no particular direction, up and down river. The
trout slip onto the banks and offer me words of
encouragement, saying *River, yes, always river.*

THE END OF THE LONG SEASON

We have waded through salal and vines
into the centre of summer. I collect
thorns and count withered berries,
the dust dries your feet, and settles
into the cracks of our bodies.
We walk on the rocks above the drought,
end by the lakeshore, walk
out of the dark of the season
into shelter.

Before it is all over, you and I
run down to the lake
with a bucket, scooping up the path
of the setting sun, and return to
our cabin. The light from the waters
keeps us warm all winter.

AS I'M TALKING TO YOU

The wind blows birds
into the edge
of my vision, golden
birds sparking
up beside me, and I try to
describe them to you;
my voice cracks
and the birds are something
I only seem to remember.

SKY IS THAT MOMENT

The sky is that moment—black blue against the
black trees, between twilight and full night.
Love, you and I are where we always are:
in our house where you light the candles while
I am at the window, closing the curtains
behind me; or on the mountain you fight
to build a camp fire as I turn, glad
that rain has left the wood damp;
or yet on the trail between home
and mountain and you're angry that I
have wandered and kept us walking after
the sun has gone down. Still here we are, love,
between twilight and full night, waiting
for the first star to spark in the darkness.

EDGE

Between gasps of metallic air
we call to the roaming whitecaps
of the strait. The waves below
undermine us, and pull at our feet,
as though we are rooted here.

The sun reflects us
in the thick waves of cloud,
we call and call,
our voices hoarse, torn, their
sound thinning, gull's cries.

You have watched it all,
seen my children
tear at each other and die,
and still they bleed.
You have told me to present you
with my dead; they are here.
You cannot carry them
from the bare stage floor.

Now what can you take from me?
I am as exposed and transfigured
as a single tree spotlit
by a shift in cloud.
Take what you can
take my dead and my years.
Leave me nothing. I fade
as the clouds shift again.

CORRESPONDENCE

This is the letter you will
write when I've gone.
You will tell me how the seasons
change without me, how
the leaves burn off the trees,
how the branches hunger
all winter, how they shake
in the wind till the famine
is over, how then the new
leaves break with light. I
will write and tell you
how nothing is different, how
this is the place
and you the man
I have neither left nor found.

HOLDING

On the day I lost my language
I took a piece of wood
and read its grain,
travelled until I stood
where it grew.

Building a pyre
I burnt
all the books of my language.
When I inhaled their smoke
they grew within me,
I became cedar, wordheavy,
and weighted with the cries
of birds.

The deer pass
but rarely approach me;
I carry the scent
of smoke and words.
Still, I gather their tracks
like twigs to use
as roots in the soil,
holding fast to the earth
that swallows me.

It is built
of wood and stone,
and has no doors,
simply windows for the wind
to knock against,
to climb in and out of:
windows into several worlds.

The weather each day
follows the last:
wind chill, the air
a sudden shower.

Bits of fir
and cedar gather
in the cracks between
the floorboards
and grow.

The wind is a highway
that plants here
all that it carries
and drifts on.
Cedar, fir, ocean,
and the scent of rain
inhabit this house.

The wind is a highway
that dropped me here
long ago, this house
a crossroad
without direction.

Two

THE SEASONS BREAK THEIR SHAPES

I am old enough now
not to think of days
but of the shapes of them.

The moon is full.
Walking for such a short time
in the forest today
I felt everything large
was there. Tonight
the clouds are patterns
of rippled sand.
I am waiting for the stars to fall
but I cannot see them.

Even the stars
were falling. The sky moved
with such great age and form
that we moved with it.

The moon is large and bright.
I can't see the sky moving
and there is only me, still, and below.
The winds are shifting
and the rain begins.

All night we continually awoke
from our dreams of falling
and flying. It was the two movements:
the slow and deep shift of the sky,
then the sharp burst of stars
against the air.

This morning I awoke
to find my hands against
the warm trunks of the cedars.
The rain was around me like dust.

There are no obvious landmarks
in any direction.

PHOTOGRAPH

I have a photograph of a child
that is my mother, my grandmother,
and me. It has that light brown hair,
round face, the same smile.
I have odd objects that hold something of
my grandmother: silver candlesticks,
handkerchiefs, linen sheets, a silk teddy
—all worn with use and age.
When she was young she
had wanted to dance, but she
married young, was widowed young,
and lived alone. This I understand.
My mother was only eighteen
when her father died, I knew
the parallels in our lives,
and watched my father until
my nineteenth birthday (my grandmother
had been a posthumous child). My mother
married my father secretly
a year before the public ceremony.
I don't know what to do with myself,
wondering how much further
the parallels go: I'm the second daughter
of a second daughter of a
second daughter; neither dancer
nor wife—a child's face
in an aging walnut frame.

and long unacquainted
with the brush, he
images for me the ocean
in a pleasing mood, gulls
and the tide pulling at
waves, shores broken by
the wash.
        He paints me there,
carefully tracing the
broken lines of my ocean
body. I'm a mermaid with
that ocean hair, eyes deep
as the far shore, far enough
to drown a man, this man

and he sketches himself there
with charcoal, black and angular,
flirting with death from the rocks,
ready to jump or be pulled
in.

VOYAGEUR

You travel only at night
    and by water.
Sometimes I see your black form
    on the lake
and hear the faint stitching of your oars
    on the water,
then I dream of you with the cool winds
    of the night.

Sometimes I see your canoe shifting like driftwood
    in the lakeweeds,
but only during the full moon, when you visit
    your only lover.

Once I walked night-heavy
    to the shore
and watched your lover die
    a death by water.
The sight of you approaching made me choke
    on my tongue.

For hours now I dream of you rowing away
    from the darkness
into the drifting path
    of the moon.

AMAZONES & THE BIRDMEN

after Herbert Seibner

Stone women
walk heavily
in and out of dreams,
their arms raised,
their legs ponderously
carrying them
between the rooms.

They dream of men trying
to fly;
men, thin with hollow bones
like birds
lifting off.

The women are weighted
by their dream
of Bella Belle,
who hovers
over northern territories
looking like a dog's bone
thick with marrow and juice.

The man in the plane
rushes the crowd.
The women think he sounds
like a hummingbird.

Then the man
crawls beside the muse
She, a languid giantess,
he, Gulliver in Brobdingnag.
Man facing Amazone,
happy to be framed.

'SKY DARK, CLOUDLESS AND STARLESS'

I *They take lights now down to the water*

In this country the sky
is all. That first day
it led me to the pool deep
in the pines. The water glowed, reflecting
the sky, and I broke off parts of the surface
to give to the men
as mirrors.

II *Only we two have moved*

That day darkened
so early, love, you told me the sky
had fallen. Then you laughed,
and we found a warm place
away from the camp, quiet
for night.

III *Poured we libations unto each the dead*

That night each man
looking into his mirror
saw hell
and we came too late
to lead them away.
You said: Shards are luck.
Then you filled your pockets.
They were ice and fire
each burning in turn.

IV *That the body of light come forth*
                          from the body of fire

We climbed the rock
and your pockets melted
leaving a slow trail of mirrors
behind us. Watching this
I turned to see the light of the sun
as it rose.
You said: No, look, it is the sky burning.

V *Dawn stands there fixed and unmoving*

And it burnt for days, but with
such a burning there was no night
but day following day.
You took the last of the shards
from your pocket saying:
It can show me nothing more.

VI *Love, gone as lightning*

And it has ceased to burn.
If you could hear me, I would say
that this time is all silence,
as are ice and mirrors.

VII *The word is made perfect*

Sky is not sky, but cloud;
behind the cloud it is the blue
that blue is not—I mean
the sky is everything falling
onto the wind-honed branches of the pines.

FULL MOON

I begin the night knowing
something will come to me:
first comes the wind and the rain
—the wind noises like birds
in the chimney, and the rain hums
against the windows. The house creaks
as though trying to fly.
Wind and rain and the
crack of the branches outside—
things lost to the tongue.

He comes from all directions.
First the wind is from the north;
the trees shudder under the weight
of the snow. He stumbles through your
doorway, shaking clumps of twigs
and snow. His eyes are ice-blue,
clear, the way the sky will be tomorrow.
His breath is cold
as the wind in your face.
His first words to you: This time
I stay. You are not ready
to believe, you offer him
a place by the fire
and not your bed, but
already his clothes melt
on your floor.
At the doorway, later, he swears
he'll be back when the wind
changes. He hands you a stone
made of ice, which you throw
in the fire as he disappears,
only days later the stone
has not melted.

From the east the wind
brings him with the stink
and push of cities. Tossing smog
from his hair, he walks
down the hill to your house
and pushes the brush
from him as he would
strangers. He stares at you
through the open window,
saying he's left it all behind.
He smells of too many
other women, and climbing
through the window he tells you
that only your flesh will wash
the scent from him. Though
the smell sickens you,
it is too hard to tell him
to leave when you know he's
already leaving.
The wind turns and the stone
he's left spreads the grime
of cities all through your house.

And he's back again
with the wind from the south
moving slowly now as though
the heat has drawn all
the winter from him. He
doesn't say a word and
your clothes fall from you
like birds. His eyes
hold yours too closely;
you aren't surprised
when everything happens
at once, but slowly,
and it almost lasts forever
in the languid night.
In the morning you wake
as slowly as you fell asleep.
He's left one flower for your hair,
and one stone.
As you move through your house that day
the new stone in your pocket
rubs against your thighs
warm and breathing
like some small animal.

If the wind is from the west
you have pockets full
of shells and sand.
He asks who you are:
you tell him the wind's name
and he takes it for his own,
pockets it like a talisman.
He tells you he never had a name,
that he is come from the same
western wind, that he has pockets
of shells and names his fingers
sift through.
It is not that you have
something he wants, but that
you are his stranger: in place
of his hands he gives you pebbles
to weigh your pockets and hold
you there. He tells you
he will stay
until you are his lover
and already you are left
holding only a small stone
turning it over.

CASSANDRA

Their eyes follow my eyes
then lose me
as I am washed into the stream of darkness
inside the hollowness inside the wood
beyond and inside the door.

Dreams come to me, like
parables of fire: I burn
before the door, with the moon
above my left shoulder, a bird
cupped in my right hand,
my arm scarred by its claws.
My eyes are white as ice, they
carry me through that door.
I have messages I must leave
to the people behind, but

inside the darkness the door seals
and I am complete:
my enclosed words
have a heartbeat, more powerful
than discourse, pulsing
through my eyes.

ST. MAUDLIN (LA FOLLE)

This is the poem
of the woman she is;
twice I have run from it.

She tries to lose herself in things,
to struggle out
and back here.

To hide herself, she has
taken a new name, but
it fits more closely than a lover.

I began this poem
for all the madwomen I know:
she is the only one.

The amazing distance:
all the years
she has travelled to come to this;
I meant to write in praise of it,
but the distance she has come to is
only the edge.

It is this thin edge that she
travels, where I don't know
on which side she has fallen;
whether she has fallen into herself,
or to madness, or if she has fallen
into the distance she's travelled —

Her body aches for one more man,
the right man.

I meant to learn to live alone,
to learn not to confuse
waking and sleeping (dreaming
of walking in white
through the green forest;
meeting a lover there).

Break her. Find her another end
than this.

Three

SEVEN ROBINS

It's the weather
they try to rest from.

It's as much January they
stiffen their wings against
as the wind.

These birds don't fly
in this weather, rather
they throw themselves
to the distance
and rest in the trees.

The dogwood, its premature
buds choked in snow,
presses these seven birds
against blowing sky;
it offers only a cold perch
and an iron rim of snow.

It's the weather I try
to rest from while I count
the birds on the tree,
and the number they are
holds them there.

In a flash and tangle
of wings, two dart away,
but two burst in from the south
and they are complete again.

The snow marks every tree.
Rattling down from the upper
branches it frightens
three more birds toward the dogwood
and three fly away.

The number they are
holds them there.

It is only an hour later
I think to look again:
and of course they have all left
in the winds that have brought on
more snow.

This is the first step—my foot
resting on what is not quite
dry land, nor air surrounding
me: cloud and sky, wind and soil.
I begin to understand
these sudden differences.
The first step and I walk
toward the eagle that is
less bird than winter: I should
mention the lack of snow, and
the mild, barely chill weather,
and the rain. This has brought him
here from wherever it is
he comes.
                    The eagle on the
dying or dead branch, neither
resting nor flying. We both
take the step from this time to
shelter. This eagle is the
first step into myself, I
who am the eagle in rain.

II

The second step comes to me
by surprise. I am off guard
and the eagle flies at me,
he stops at my eye level
and I know now that he moves
straight ahead, inside. The earth
rolls beneath me, twists away
from my feet (or is it I,
turning?) This is the eagle
that I know too well, the one
flying through me, the eagle
with his tense claws on my heart.

III

The last step is the eagle
I see from above, the one
spread out below me, like an
offering, like a hunter.

He just dove for prey, a small
animal screaming in the
old grass. As I watch he is
smaller than the smallest prey,
older than the grass, and more
hollow from this uncertain
angle I ride. I am old
and tired, hollow-boned and dry.

If this is the fourth step, the
eagle is farther below
me, the wind pulling at me,
and I spot the eagle as
he does his prey. The eagles
are what I see or what I
think I see. Charcoal moving
in burning fields.

The strangers are those
     who live here, those
     on the coast
     and this island.
Each one is a traveller,
     each moves without
     recognition through
     the familiar land.
They walk the forests
     without submission.
     Only strangers
     can do that.

                    *

It is winter now, inextricably
     the first winter I spent here,
     and the last, and
     the one I live now.

                    *

It was this year,
     or last, that I saw the whale,
     scarred by all the years
     he had lived here,
he rolled slowly against
     the deep surf
     of the beach. This is his island;
     he is old enough to claim it.
He turned slowly in waves,
     marking the shore
     with the thick
     black log of his body.

It must be last year
        that I walked to the edge
        of the cliff, trying to find
        an end to the island.
I stood above the beach where
        I had seen the whale,
        and breathed the grey light
        of winter dawn.
A large black husk
        suddenly flew at me,
        missing me
        by inches.
I had never seen
        an owl here before,
        I had only heard them in the dark,
        searching for the end of the land.

It must be this year
        I saw the bald eagle
        fighting the wind
        in a bare alder by the road,
hunched, angry,
        at the thin branch,
        the strong wind,
        the traffic pulling below.

                    *

I knew then
        this land is a branch
        that doesn't quite
        hold me.

HAWK

Everything is an omen:
the shapes of clouds,
the turn of leaves,
twigs falling together
in a certain pattern,
even the twist of the sun
through the branches
has a particular meaning.
I try to know exactly
how to interpret these
signs, but don't know
what to think as I see
the hawk I was watching
fall.

ECHOES

It escapes you:
this connection
between two moments
of repeating time is something
other than déjà vu,
a continuous time.

*

See the hawk on the wheel-
edge, turning farther from shore
taunted by a pair of gulls,
becoming bird, then speck,
then bird again, fainter and

remember driving home through
the frost fog, through suburbs
then bursting through the trees,
the shoreline and road curving together,
the ocean lost, but shadowing
the road again. The ocean curves
as if at high tide it would
sweep the road.

*

It is coming together and gone,
those moments of loss and gain,
of time coming back
and back.

ISLAND FOREST

1 The Forest by Day

Suddenly the wind spins
in the wood, and throws me
back against the trees as though
pushing me aside. The forest
has memories it wants
to play back to itself
and I am the intruder.
The forest recalls when
it wasn't a forest,
when it was only part of
the land, stretching the length
of the island. One wood,
one island.
            The wind
pushes my hair against my eyes
with cold and deliberate fingers,
and no amount of smoothing
keeps it back. I close my
eyes, take a step forward and the wind
butts against me. Though I'm
still standing I have lost my balance;
vertigo rocks my head
like the branches. I step back
to lean against the solid trunks,
but they are less solid now,
and I'm gasping for air. There's too
much of it—too much wind
pushing against my body and filling
my head. Too much of the forest
around me, taking me back with
itself, and I walk out into calmer
weather, with threads of a memory
not mine to haunt me.

II From my own Backyard

This is the first time
I have written you
from here. My back yard
is a tangle of fallen fir
and cedar, and now
I write to tell you
my own fall is as fruitful:
from my side
the rain is drawing moss
and flowering weeds.

III A Breath of Rain

The winter rains have strayed into
the spring.

In this ocean of rain and air
that tastes thickly of leaves,
the forest sinks around me.
Roots stretch more deeply
into the soil, but
cedars begin to sway,
and land, broken, onto
the film of leaves.
The thimbleberries, the salal
finally grow green;
I push my way
through this.

The snake fence is beginning
to ease down the hill to the road.
Only yards below it
the car door waits, rusting.
The seats, too,
are left, they sit deeper
in the forest, bounded by
fallen cedar. The pornographic
pages of a magazine rot
below a tree whose entire
east side aches with sap.
I lost my balance there,
and have to lean against
that tree.

I used to walk along these logs.
Now I see the moss is heavier,
somehow greener on them,
and they are slippery with rain
and hollow. The trilliums
are in virginal bloom
in the decaying leaves.
The bush tightens around me
in the clearing.

I push my way through
this; around me
the forest crumbles.

SIMILKAMEEN

for Harold & Diane

This is to tell you
that I have not forgotten.
You told me how time moves
in blocks of light as memory,
hazing in front of your mountains.
I will not forget.

When I visit you
I never arrive: the river
pushes me out of the valley
back to the coast.
Still, the Similkameen
grows in you,
like dust and poems;
here the rainforest
thickens me with language.

Now I tell you
each sunrise multiplies
by three: memory
split by the lightning
from the ridges.
You have been there;
are there;
will be there still.
We multiply
and are parted.

ANY WEATHER

Try the weather—it
at least
is something to walk
into. It's something
like morning or
like rain when you
taste it. When your
skin tastes it.
This weather
is a continual
revision. Cutting
ideas down to size.
I couldn't resist
adding that.
But the light, yes,
it's something
central, even
in November when it's
more the rain
that burns.

NOVEMBER ARRIVES ON THE COAST

It is not the rain that leaves
me here, not that this place
can hold me with its gray wind,
but something about the turning
of the year into a new season
makes me stay to watch what remains.

It is not that much remains,
I saw that almost everything leaves.
When the rain brings on this season,
the year become an empty place
and the scraps of the days are turning
in the anger of the thickening wind.

I keep changing with the wind;
I feel the fear that remains
when the year begins turning
against me, when all the leaves
set out for another place,
and I am alone with the season.

But this is my season
and not even the strength of the wind
can blow me from this place.
I am what remains
when all else leaves
—the only thing not turning.

The landscape never begins turning
real or concrete. It will only season
the air with all the colours of leaves
carried in the dense wind
that carries all the remains
from this, into another place.

I grow deeper: here I find a place
that is mine alone. I am turning
into a tree that remains
even now, in this season.
I draw back from the wind,
but it is never me that leaves.

This is the place where the leaves
are turning in the northern wind,
where the remains of the year turn into a season.

if you want to touch a cedar
take a few steps backward
give it a chance
to get a good look at you
if at that point it does not
turn tail and
disappear into the woods
do not think you have it made
but take only
a few cautious forward steps
make no sudden moves
give it a chance
to see if it likes you closer up
when you are at arm's length
reach out and touch it gently
if it does not shudder
(and if you do not)
wrap your arms around it
in a hug
and cling there

These are strange forests
wetter and wilder
than any other
on the coast,
marshy lands
where the trees are
shrouded in moss
and the light
filters greener
than any water.
It is safer here
not to tread
off the boardwalk:
the soil here
is not to be trusted
to bear a man's weight,
and is kind only
to women who
carry children.
If you want to
touch a cedar
stay on the boardwalk,
touch wood
and run.
Hear the forest thudding
after you.

IV The Road at Midnight

I must be dreaming this
bending rising pouring
of myself over the road
through the forest.
Each corner is a cliff
I fall through.

v Back in the Woods

Suddenly it is quiet, and the night
has landed in the middle of
itself. The winds no longer claw
at the full moon as if to draw blood;
the silence makes me uneasy,
moves almost perceptibly, is
a dark void pulling the woods
into itself. This is
a moment you must
live to understand, when
you stand at attention in wonder
at yourself, making the decision
whether to jump or hold on.
I have chosen
not to fall to silence, but to arm
myself against it, and to join
the conspiracy of filling
the silences, never allowing them
to join one with the other until
all language is the punctuation
of the silences, till the forest is what
fills the void in itself; rather now
it must be the lapse
that punctuates our syllables:
the blessing of a constant
wind in the dying forest.

Here—
this is another darkness,
another silence
growing between my words
and the deep, still air.

This is the new world.
The sun rises anywhere here;
as you read the weather
I read your hesitations
I say: Let's burn the black fir,
and raise our children beside the ashes.

We are growing silence;
we are growing light.

Here—
this is morning,
this is the building
of light for the new land.
(The sea
gathers the sun
in a whisper.)

It's amazing how we never walk from a room
but the doorway follows us to the next.

Amazing that it's the same doorway.
Amazing that I am through.

Still more that the word is a maze,
no, a labyrinth, the minotaur (its meaning)

tears at everything
moving down the corridor.

The door to the hall is open,
my light gets through to the dark hall.

There are cats in the dark outside.
There are forests there.

I can light a candle with my words.
I can as quickly blow the flame away.

I blow the flame deep into the labyrinth,
set a spark onto the end of the bull's tail,

hear him below for miles and years.
I look out into the hall,

and see only a reflection of my own light;
it's like walking through the labyrinth

and finding the passage isn't the passage out,
it is only the passage farther in;

they are all only passages farther in
and the wind has blown

the flame from our candles.

CONTENTS

One

Two

Three

ACKNOWLEDGEMENTS

Some of these poems have appeared in *The Antigonish Review*,
the *Anthology of Magazine Verse & Yearbook of American
Poetry* (U.S.A.), *CutBank* (U.S.A.), *The Fiddlehead, From an
Island, Island, The Malahat Review, Student Oracle, The
Wascana Review, WOT*, and the booklet, *Travelling in Place*
with Harold Rhenisch.

The italicized lines in the poem 'Sky Dark, Cloudless and
Starless,' including the title, are borrowed from Pound's
Cantos.

Love and thanks to John Barton, Harold Rhenisch, and Jim
and Greg for their editorial help.

RECENT TITLES IN THE PENUMBRA PRESS POETRY SERIES

ANN FOX CHANDONNET *Auras Tendrils (Poems of the North)*
    ISBN 0 920806 45 7

DEBORAH GODIN *Stranded in Terra*
    ISBN 0 920806 53 8

MARY WEYMARK GOSS *In Hiding*
    ISBN 0 920806 54 6

NEILE GRAHAM *Seven Robins*
    ISBN 0 920806 55 4

M.T. KELLY *Country You Can't Walk In and Other Poems*
    ISBN 0 920806 56 2

ELIZABETH KOUHI *Round Trip Home*
    ISBN 0 920806 57 0

J. MICHAEL YATES *Insel: The Queen Charlotte Islands Meditations*
    ISBN 0 920806 58 9

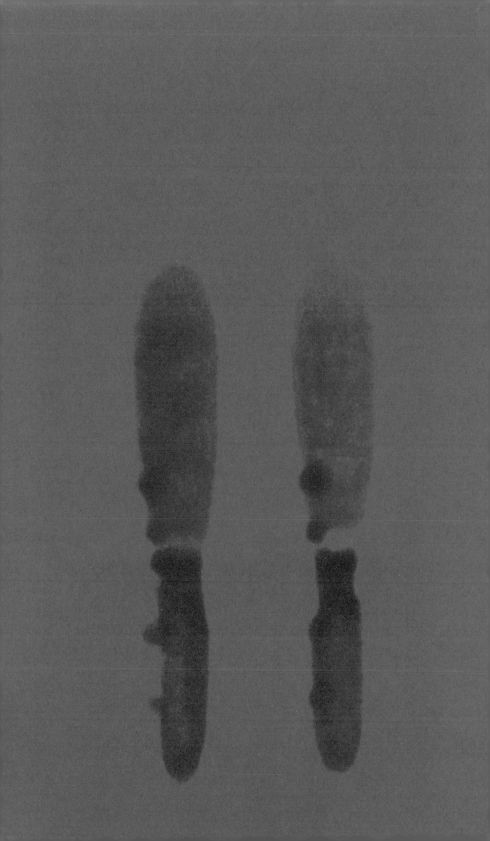

DATE DUE